75

PICTURE PROMPTS
FOR YOUNG WRITERS

BY RICK BROWN

S C H O L A S T I C
PROFESSIONAL **B**OOKS

New York•Toronto•London•Auckland•Sydney

W9-CFH-440

Scholastic, Inc., grants teachers permission to photocopy
the activity sheets from this book for classroom use.
No other part of this publication may be reproduced in whole or in part, or stored in a retrieval system, or transmitted in any form or by any
means, electronic, mechanical, photocopying, recording, or otherwise, without written permission of the publisher.
For information regarding permission, write to
Scholastic, Inc., 730 Broadway, New York, NY 10003.

Designed by Vincent Ceci

Cover and interior illustration by Rick Brown

ISBN 0-590-49408-2

Copyright©1993 by Scholastic, Inc. All rights reserved.

Contents

Introduction

The last time you pulled out the family photo album, didn't it open the flood gates for many memorable stories? And when you browsed through the pictures in your latest travel brochure, didn't you imagine the details of the wonderful places you'd see and the things you'd do?

Each picture you see has its own story. That is the premise on which this book is based. If "a picture paints a thousand words," then be prepared for a year full of writing. By incorporating picture prompts into your classroom writing program, you can provide a window to the world of real and imagined situations and characters.

Picture prompts can serve as a way to motivate reluctant writers or those with temporary "writer's block." By inviting these writers to imagine the "befores" and "afters" of these pictures, you can help to alleviate some of the pressure felt during writing periods.

Prompts can also provide the focus of mini-lessons on writing skills. After pinpointing a skill that needs development, begin a class story based on one of the pictures. As the story develops, draw the children's attention to the writing element you wish to teach (e.g., using specific language, spelling, correcting run-on sentences, punctuation, capitalization, and so on).

The pictures in this book can serve as an introduction to different genre forms, such as plays. (Prompts showing two characters engaged in dialogue are particularly suitable for this form.) A narrative text could be written about any of the pictures. Some others lend themselves to other writing formats, including poetry, jokes, newspaper articles, recipes, and menus. The only limit is your students' and your imagination!

In writing about the pictures, students may need to call on vocabulary words that are not commonly used in story writing. Menus and recipes require different words than jokes and poems. By developing a list of appropriate words for various writing situations, the prompts spark a valuable class activity.

Do some of the pictures remind you of a story you've read to the class? Then use them to enrich and extend literary experiences! The resulting children's stories can imitate known story lines and still be unique and original, based on the student writers' own experiences and voices.

Oral expression is a part of the language arts experience that may be overlooked as a tool in the writing process. By using these picture prompts to generate discussions, children have the chance to create, develop, talk about, and think through story ideas.

By sharing these picture prompts with your students, you may unlock the treasure chest of mental pictures each one carries inside— memories and experiences that they may share with you in future, as they continue to develop as students and as writers.

How To Use This Book

There are as many way to use the reproducible prompts in this book as there are teachers and teaching styles. However, a few general suggestions will get you started.

You may wish to reproduce one prompt at a time in sufficient quantity for every child to have her own. Or, you may reproduce prompts on sheets of acetate for use on an overhead projector. They are suitable for group or individual student use. Students may want to color the pictures, or add themselves to the scenes before or after writing.

The prompts are loosely divided into categories according to subject matter, from *Friends Together*, to *Something Strange.* Each chapter opens with specific suggestions keyed to individual prompts within that chapter.

With any of the prompts, start by inviting the children to look closely at the picture and talk about what they see. What do they think is happening? What might have happened right before this picture? What might happen next? What is unusual or different about this picture? and so on. Then you may wish to lead them to create poems, menus, recipes, dialogues, or narratives, as the individual prompts suggest.

Students may wish to color the pictures, draw themselves into the scenes, or extend the prompts by adding their own pictures, and stapling them to the ready-made prompts to make a book. Allow your students' creativity free rein, and watch their writing blossom!

Part 1

Friends Together

When friends get together, all kinds of things can happen. There are many stories to be told from the prompts in this section. There are ways to tie in math and science, too. Here are some individual suggestions to get you started:

Kids can:

page 9
Write a book listing all the different kinds of pies they can think of, write an alphabet book of favorite or imagined pies, or make a graph of the class's favorite pies.

page 10
List and discuss solutions to this problem, including how the window will be paid for.

page 11
Relate the story as a mathematical word problem.

page 12
Make a literature tie-in: *Scary Stories to Tell in the Dark,* by Alvin Schwartz, HarperCollins.

page 13
Participate in a cooking lesson with the class; discuss cookbook language; write your own class recipes, cookbook.

Friends Together

Name _____

_____

_____

_____

_____

_____

_____

_____

Name _____

_____

_____

_____

_____

_____

_____

_____

Name _____

_____

_____

_____

_____

_____

_____

_____

Name _____

_____

_____

_____

_____

_____

_____

Name _____

_____

_____

_____

_____

_____

_____

_____

Friends Together

Name _____

_____

_____

_____

_____

_____

_____

_____

Name _____

_____

_____

_____

_____

_____

_____

_____

Friends Together

Name _____

_____

_____

_____

_____

_____

_____

_____

_____

Part 2

Far-Out Fun

There's plenty of fun ahead—
a chance to imagine some exciting and unusual situations!

Kids can:

pages 16 and 17
Discuss the history of early flight; describe how to build a "flying machine."

page 19
Discuss cause and effect.

pages 20, 21,and 22
Think about: what laws of nature are being broken here?

Far-Out Fun

Name _____

_____

_____

_____

_____

_____

_____

_____

_____

Name _____

_____
_____
_____
_____
_____
_____
_____
_____

Name _____

Name _____

_____

_____

_____

_____

_____

_____

_____

_____

_____

_____

Far-Out Fun

Name _____

_____

_____

_____

_____

_____

_____

_____

_____

Far-Out Fun

Name _____

_____

_____

_____

_____

_____

_____

_____

Far-Out Fun

Name _____

_____

_____

_____

_____

_____

_____

_____

Far-Out Fun

Name _____

_____
_____
_____
_____
_____
_____
_____

Part 3

Home Sweet Home

There's certainly no place like the homes in these prompts! Unusual happenings in familiar settings should spark your students' creativity!

Kids can:

page 25
Use this picture as the start of a bulletin board on which children's writing and illustrations about dreams can be displayed.

page 26
Tie into the science program by writing about wind-powered vehicles.

page 27
Use word bubbles to describe what each character is thinking; what each character should do next?

page 28
Write a recipe for the world's biggest chocolate chip cookie (pizza, birthday cake, bagel, etc.) .

Home Sweet Home

Name _____

_____

_____

_____

_____

_____

_____

Home Sweet Home

Name _____

_____

_____

_____

_____

_____

_____

_____

_____

_____

Home Sweet Home

Name _____

_____

_____

_____

_____

_____

_____

_____

Home Sweet Home

Name

Part 4

Animal Antics

Animals seem to "bring out the *best*" in kids and their writing. The prompts in this section are sure to provide some fun!

Kids can:

page 30
Use synonyms for "big" to describe the dog.

page 31
Write the pro's and con's of this or any pet.

page 32
Write a newspaper article and headline describing this species.

page 41
After identifying the animal parts, name this new creature. Draw and describe your own combination animal.

page 43
Pretend they're stranded on the island and need the dogs to rescue them.

page 44
Use drawings as well as words to tell what happens next.

page 45
Draw word balloons above the characters, and write inside them.

page 46
Explain how to play their favorite card game.

page 47
Make a literature connection to James Marshall's "George and Martha" stories.

page 48
Write directions.

page 49
Make a literature connection to "The Three Billy Goats Gruff."

page 57
Think about whether they'd be able to eat at such a place. What could humans eat here?

page 59
Think about what they might see on the menu of this cafe. Make the menu, including the dishes and their cost.

page 60
Think about what the people on the bus will say/do when the alligators get on board.

page 61
Write out a plan for the rabbits to get to the carrot without getting caught. Make a literature connection to Peter Rabbit's adventures by Beatrix Potter.

In addition pages 40 thorough 57
Write a play or a dialogue between the characters.

Animal Antics

Name _____

_____

_____

_____

_____

_____

_____

Name _____

_____

_____

_____

_____

_____

_____

_____

Animal Antics

Name _____

_____

_____

_____

_____

_____

_____

_____

Name _____

_____

_____

_____

_____

_____

_____

_____

_____

Animal Antics

Name _____

_____

_____

_____

_____

_____

_____

_____

Name _____

_____
_____
_____
_____
_____
_____
_____

Animal Antics

Name _____

_____

_____

_____

_____

_____

_____

_____

Animal Antics

Name _____

_____

_____

_____

_____

_____

_____

_____

Animal Antics

Name _____

_____

_____

_____

_____

_____

_____

_____

Name _____

_____

_____

_____

_____

_____

_____

_____

_____

Animal Antics

_____

_____

_____

_____

_____

_____

_____

Name _____

_____

_____

_____

_____

_____

_____

_____

Animal Antics

_____

_____

_____

_____

_____

_____

_____

Name _____

_____

_____

_____

_____

_____

_____

_____

_____

Name _____

_____

_____

_____

_____

_____

_____

_____

Name _____

_____
_____
_____
_____
_____
_____
_____

Name _____

_____

_____

_____

_____

_____

_____

_____

Animal Antics

Name _____

_____

_____

_____

_____

_____

_____

_____

_____

Animal Antics

SUBWAY

Animal Antics

Name _____

_____

_____

_____

_____

_____

_____

_____

_____

Name _____

_____

_____

_____

_____

_____

_____

_____

_____

Name _____

_____

_____

_____

_____

_____

_____

_____

Name _____

_____

_____

_____

_____

_____

_____

_____

Name _____

_____

_____

_____

_____

_____

_____

_____

Name _____

_____

_____

_____

_____

_____

_____

_____

_____

Animal Antics

Name _____

_____

_____

_____

_____

_____

_____

_____

_____

_____

Name _____

_____

_____

_____

_____

_____

_____

Name _____

_____

_____

_____

_____

_____

_____

_____

Animal Antics

Name _____

_____
_____
_____
_____
_____
_____
_____
_____

Name _____

_____

_____

_____

_____

_____

_____

_____

Animal Antics

Name _____

_____

_____

_____

_____

_____

_____

_____

_____

Name _____

Name _____

_____

_____

_____

_____

_____

_____

Part 5

Something Strange

Do these characters and situations remind you of stories you've read? Use these pictures to tie into your literature program. Strange creatures also provide great art projects and bulletin board displays when you add writing and more illustrations.

Kids can:

page 64
Write a scientific formula for growing the world's biggest pumpkin.

page 65
Draw and describe what comes out of the spaceship. What happens next?

page 66
Write the dialogue for the creature and the other party on the line.

page 67
Pretend to be the captain and write a logbook entry for this day,
when a sea serpent appeared.

page 68
Relate to a theme unit on the ocean. Draw similarly named sea creatures:
e.g., sea horse, starfish, sunfish, etc.

page 69
Read and discuss "wish stories," like *Ali Baba and the Forty Thieves, Aladdin,*
or *The Fisherman and His Wife.*

page 70
Write about what the farmers will do with such a big strawberry.

page 71
Make a literature connection to Mercer Mayer's *There's a Nightmare in my Closet.*

page 72
As an art activity, make trees of their favorite things, and describe how they grow.

page 74
Make a literature connection to *Beauty and the Beast.*

Something Strange

Name _____

_____
_____
_____
_____
_____
_____
_____

Something Strange

Name _____

_____
_____
_____
_____
_____
_____
_____
_____
_____

Something Strange

Name _____

_____

_____

_____

_____

_____

_____

_____

Something Strange

Name _____

Name _____

_____

_____

_____

_____

_____

_____

_____

_____

Something Strange

_____

_____

_____

_____

_____

_____

_____

Name _____

Name _____

_____
_____
_____
_____
_____
_____
_____
_____

Something Strange

Name _____

_____

_____

_____

_____

_____

_____

_____

Name _____

_____
_____
_____
_____
_____
_____
_____
_____
_____
_____

Something Strange

Name _____

Something Strange

Name _____

_____

_____

_____

_____

_____

_____

_____

_____

Something Strange

Name _____

Something Strange

Something Strange

Name _____

_____

_____

_____

_____

_____

_____

_____

Something Strange

_____

_____

_____

_____

_____

_____

_____

Something Strange

_____

_____

_____

_____

_____

_____

_____

_____

_____

_____

_____

Something Strange

Name _____

_____

_____

_____

_____

_____

_____

_____

_____

Something Strange

_____

_____

_____

_____

_____

_____

_____

_____

Something Strange

Name _____

_____

_____

_____

_____

_____

_____

_____

_____

Something Strange

Name _____

_____
_____
_____
_____
_____
_____
_____

Create-a-Prompt

Name

Create-a-Prompt

Name _____

_____

_____

_____

_____

_____

_____

_____

Create-a-Prompt

Name _____

_____

_____

_____

_____

_____

_____

_____